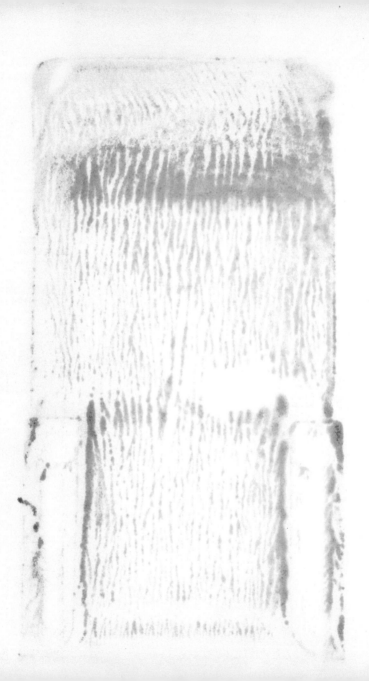

ESSENTIALS

OF

PARLIAMENTARY PROCEDURE

THIRD EDITION

J. Jeffery Auer

Key to Contents

Key to Contents

ESSENTIALS

of

PARLIAMENTARY PROCEDURE

By
J. JEFFERY AUER
INDIANA UNIVERSITY

THIRD EDITION

APPLETON-CENTURY-CROFTS, INC.
NEW YORK

For JOHN Q. DOAKES

who may someday take part
in or preside over a
business meeting

PREFACE

Will Rogers once said that "whenever two Americans meet on the street, one of them pounds a gavel and calls the meeting to order." Exaggerated as this quip may be, we do know that the voluntary association is a striking phenomenon of American culture. A vast majority of persons in our society belong to at least one business, professional, service, or social club. As members they are obliged to take part in or to preside over business meetings of these organizations. This manual of the essentials of parliamentary procedure is designed to aid them in conducting these meetings democratically and efficiently. It is not intended as a mere simplification of Robert's *Rules of Order Revised,* although it is compatible with them throughout. It presents concisely only the *essentials* of parliamentary procedure.

J. JEFFERY AUER

INTRODUCTION

"In a system of well-digested rules . . . will be found the only buckler of defense that reflection can have against precipitancy, moderation against violence, modesty against arrogance, veracity against falsehood, simplicity against deception and intrigue."— Jeremy Bentham, *Essay on Political Tactics*.

It is sometimes facetiously said of the theatre director that his main reason for being is to keep people from running into each other on the stage. The same might be said for the presiding officer and the parliamentarian: their purpose, and that of the parliamentary procedure they employ, is to keep individual members of the large discussion group from running into each other, figuratively, at least, as they seek solutions for their common problems. There should be nothing mysterious about parliamentary procedure; it is simply a standardized code of everyday good manners applied to the special situation created when a large number of people gather together in a business meeting to take some form of group action. This code of good manners is both democratic and efficient: (1) democratic in that it provides for the rule of the majority at the same time that it protects the rights of the minority, and (2) efficient in that while it provides for full and free discussion of all matters it limits group consideration to but one subject at a time and requires an orderly disposition of each item of business before taking up another.

1

Since the time of men's earliest associations the need for some code of parliamentary good manners has always been recognized. When that need has not been met, democracy has frequently been the first casualty. Many historians believe that the excesses of the Legislative Assembly in the French Revolution may be attributed to the "lamentable consequences of a want of knowledge in managing the debates and rules of order. . . ." The same is true of any deliberative assembly, whether it be a national legislature, a corporate board of directors, or the business meeting of a local service club: with power to act but no standard of procedure, the result is likely to be reckless and aimless action.

It is equally true, of course, that when any group adopts a set code of parliamentary procedure, some restraints are inevitably put upon individual action. Such restraints may be justified if they operate for the common good: "when there is no law, but every man does what is right in his own eyes, there is the least of real liberty."

This real significance of parliamentary rules is often ignored, unhappily, by overly zealous devotees of "the discussion method." They assert that "parliamentary rules have functioned for years to stymie meetings . . . they make it possible for a few to take control. . . . Certain tricks of parliamentary procedure are favorite weapons for confusing issues and raising doubt. . . . The rules for discussion should be almost the complete opposite of Robert's *Rules of Order*."

Such comments do less than justice to Colonel Robert who wrote in *Parliamentary Practice:* "One who is constantly raising points of order and insisting upon the strict observance of every rule in a peaceable assembly in which most of the members are ignorant of these rules and customs, makes himself a nuisance, hinders business, and prejudices people against parliamentary law. Such a person is either ignorant of its real purpose or else willfully misuses his knowledge." We note in passing that ignoring parliamentary rules does not inevitably result in good discussion. Indeed, we would even defend the use of parliamentary procedures for obstructionist purposes in a situation where an arbitrary or unscrupulous group attempts to force hasty or ill-considered action by the "steam-roller" method. To delay final action until there has been free and ample discussion is a legitimate use of parliamentary procedure.

Even the fact that rules can be misused does not mean that they should be abolished, for "without discipline, public spirit stands as poor a chance in a numerous assembly as valor in the field." As Robert says, ". . . if each member could talk on any subject as long as he pleased and as many times as he pleases, and if all could talk at the same time it would be impracticable in most cases to ascertain their deliberate judgment on any particular matter." In short, parliamentary rules are just as necessary, and no more technical, than rules governing baseball or football.

The main objectives of parliamentary rules are to guard against hasty, ill-considered action, to give each member an equal right to be heard, to determine the will of the majority, and to protect the rights of the minority. Hence these sensible principles govern discussion and debate in business meetings:

1. Only one question can be considered at a time. It must be properly phrased, moved by one member, seconded by another, and then thrown open for discussion and debate. Similarly, only one amendment can be considered at a time.
2. No one can speak until he has risen, addressed the presiding officer, and been "recognized."

3. No one can speak a second time on the same question as long as another wants to speak for his first time.
4. When two or more members rise to speak, the chairman should recognize one who opposes the preceding speaker, and preferably one who has not spoken previously.

We emphasize that these are principles governing *business* meetings, for it is our judgment that many who criticize parliamentary procedure do so because they overlook the distinction made by Colonel Robert and other parliamentarians between rules for small committee meetings and those for business meetings of large organizations. Committee meetings very properly employ the discussion method. They are usually quite informal. Members do not rise and address the chair. They can speak as often as they please provided they do not deprive other members of opportunities to present their views. The chairman may take an active part in the discussion, and he may put questions to a vote on his own initiative after an informal discussion. He should feel free to try to achieve a consensus. "In all cases," says Robert, "efforts should be made to obtain a unanimous report." The opportunity for just this kind of informal discussion is provided by parliamentary law. If members of an organization wish to consider a question informally, someone moves that "we discuss the problem of XYZ informally," or that they meet as a "committee of the whole" for a specified period and purpose. In such a committee, noncontroversial matters may be passed by unanimous consent.

Parliamentary procedure, however, is the best method yet devised for taking action on controversial issues in business meetings, whether of legislatures or weekly luncheon clubs. There are rules for hastening action when something must be done immediately. There are also ways of delaying action for

various reasons. Ultimately, however, in our form of government, there comes a time when legislators must stand up and
be counted. Then the will of the majority, or sometimes of
two-thirds of those present, becomes law. The minority must
abide by that decision while leaders of the "loyal opposition"
lay plans to reverse the decision at the next session. The same
procedure, adapted to the needs of the group, applies to our
clubs and organizations; the secretary's minutes, when read
and approved, are the legal record.

It is essential, of course, that parliamentary procedures be
adapted to the needs of each group using them. As in the case
of good social manners, certain parliamentary situations are
most comfortably met by those who are familiar with well-
ordered and universal forms, forms that are customary largely
because of their convenience. But, as acceptable codes of eti-
quette may vary from one community to another, we should
recognize that appropriate codes for conducting business meetings may vary from one organization to another. The following
generalizations may be helpful in determining the degree to
which parliamentary rules should be followed in business meetings of different clubs and organizations. Greater use should be
made of formal parliamentary procedures when the membership is relatively large, when the group's purpose is action
rather than exploration, when the division of opinions is sharp,
when a relatively high degree of formality is desired, and when
members of the group are familiar with parliamentary rules.

We have said that democracy and parliamentary procedure
invariably accompany each other. Indeed, the term *parliamentary law*, itself, indicates its democratic origins, for it is derived
from the rules and customs of conducting business in the
British Parliament. These usages in turn provided the basis
for the earliest procedures followed in the United States Senate,

originally drafted by Thomas Jefferson who undertook, as he
said, "a sketch, which those who come after me will successively
correct and fill up, till a code of rules shall be formed for the
use of the Senate, the effects of which may be accuracy of business, economy of time, order, uniformity and impartiality." The
general practices of the British Parliament and the American
Congress were the sources upon which Colonel Henry M.
Robert drew when he devised a parliamentary code in 1876,
still considered as "the parliamentarian's Bible." In the constitutions of many organizations today, it is established that
"for all questions of parliamentary procedure Robert's *Rules of
Order Revised* will be considered authoritative." Thus the present manual, and any other like it, is derived from a long tradi-
tion of democratic practice in the conduct of business meetings.

It is precisely because Robert's rules are in the direct line of
descent from British and American legislative bodies, however, that they seem so encyclopedic. Their number and com-
plexity frequently confuse and frustrate the ordinary layman
whose only desire is to dispose of the business of his club, lodge,
or board with efficiency and dispatch. Thus the average citizen,
businessman or clubwoman, too often concludes that "parliamentarians are pettifoggers," hampering rather than expediting
this process. It is for such persons that this manual is written. It
contains, we hope, only the *essentials* of parliamentary procedure, a simple and succinct code of good manners to be applied to the business of everyday group meetings. It takes for
granted that parliamentary rules are but a means to an end
and not an end in themselves; as with all good governing regulations, it supposes that laws are for men and not men for laws.
Therefore this manual outlines standardized but simplified procedures, assuming that any individual organization will make

such additions or exceptions as its own peculiar character requires.

Part I, "The Organization and Conduct of Meetings," defines and describes the general stages through which a group meeting progresses from the time it is called to order by the chairman until it is adjourned, and the more common parliamentary devices which expedite the transaction of business in orderly fashion. The arrangement of this section is a functional one, treating consecutively each stage of a business meeting.

Part II, "Special Motions," deals with parliamentary procedures designed for particular purposes or to meet specific situations often arising in typical business meetings. Because the exercise of courtesy and common sense may often obviate the need to apply a special motion, the total number of these has been kept to a minimum. While even some of these will be employed infrequently, the association member should be familiar with them all. The arrangement of this section is also functional, with the special motions grouped according to purpose.

Part III, "Precedence of Motions," takes up the problem of assigning priorities among special motions which may be proposed concurrently.

Part IV, "Duties of the Presiding Officer," summarizes the role and function of the chairman of a business meeting.

Part V, "Constitutions and Bylaws," presents a brief outline of common elements in the rules of voluntary associations.

Part VI, "Suggested Readings," consists of recommended sources for more extensive study of parliamentary procedure.

I

THE ORGANIZATION AND CONDUCT OF MEETINGS

A. CALL TO ORDER

When the members of a group have assembled and the appointed time has arrived, the chairman (or the temporary chairman in an initial meeting of a conference or a convention) calls the meeting to order, usually with the simple request: *"Will the meeting please come to order?"* Where neither officers nor a temporary chairman have been named, the person who issued the "call" for the meeting usually calls the meeting to order. In a large meeting where he may have difficulty in making himself heard, the chairman may reinforce his call by rapping on a table with his gavel.

The Quorum

Ordinarily this call to order will not be given by the chairman until he is fairly sure that a quorum of the group is present —a quorum being the minimum number of members necessary to transact business. The number of members making up a quorum is usually stipulated in the bylaws or the standing rules of an organization; if there is no such rule, a quorum is presumed to be a simple majority of the total membership.

If, at any time during the meeting, the absence of a quorum should be established (usually upon the request of a member for a roll call), the assembly may continue its debate but may not take any definite action other than on a motion to adjourn.

The Order of Business

From the time the chairman has called a meeting to order until its adjournment, business is conducted according to a prearranged sequence. Normally this sequence is the accepted order of business (sometimes called orders of the day), which the present discussion follows:

1. Call to order
2. Reading of the minutes of the last meeting
3. Reports of standing committees
4. Reports of special committees
5. Unfinished business from previous meetings
6. New business
7. Miscellaneous: announcements, requests, items, etc.
8. Adjournment

Rarely in voluntary associations, but sometimes in formal conventions, the rules require a roll call at the opening session. Occasionally an official host will welcome convention delegates. Some meetings are customarily opened with an invocation. Should any of these matters be appropriate, they come immediately after the call to order.

The Agenda

Sometimes, however, the agenda, or special order of business, may have been drawn up and announced in advance of the meeting, and this will take precedence over the customary order of business unless by unanimous consent of the group a particular matter is designated as a "special order of business." Such agenda might be drawn up for a convention, for example, when one entire meeting is to be devoted to the adoption of a platform or to the nomination and election of convention candidates. Or in a conference the report of a particular committee may be deemed of sufficient importance to occupy an entire session. In no case, however, should such agenda or special order of business take precedence over the reading of the minutes of the previous meeting.

B. READING OF THE MINUTES

The first item of business before a meeting, after it has come to order, is the reading of the minutes of the previous meeting by the secretary or clerk of the organization. Since the purpose of this reading of the minutes is to recall to the membership what was done at the last meeting, the only time when it may properly be omitted is at the second or third consecutive session in a single day.

Writing the Minutes

As written from his notes taken during a business meeting, the secretary's minutes are a complete and objective account of what happened at the meeting. Thus they become a permanent record, which may be referred to at some later date, of all business discussed and all action taken. Ordinarily it is not necessary to summarize the actual discussion, although every main motion, whether adopted or rejected, should be recorded, with the name of its maker. In no case should the secretary record his personal opinions in the official minutes. The minutes will, of course, state the exact time, date, and place of the meeting, the name of the presiding officer, and whether the meeting was a regular or a special one. They should be dated and signed by the secretary.

Correcting the Minutes

At the conclusion of the reading of the minutes the chairman will ask: *"Are there any corrections or additions to the minutes as read?"* If any member wishes to make such changes, he addresses the chair (which must always be the first step when a member wishes to speak) and, being recognized, makes his point. The chairman may then ask whether there is any objection to the alteration of the minutes, and, if there is none, he will order the secretary to make the necessary change. If there is an objection to a correction of the minutes, the proposed change must be stated as a motion and dealt with in the usual way.

Approving the Minutes

After this the chairman may then simply say: *"If there are no other objections, the minutes stand approved as read* [or *corrected*]*."* This procedure is far simpler, and less time-consuming, than to call for a motion proposing the adoption of the minutes, although such a procedure may be stipulated in the standing rules of some organizations.

Once the minutes have been approved, the secretary should write the word *approved* and the date of approval at the end of the minutes. Thereafter they stand as the official record of the meeting and should be available to any member who wishes to recall its business.

C. REPORTS OF STANDING COMMITTEES

In most organizations a great deal of routine business is delegated to committees; they also do much of the investigation preliminary to ultimate action by the assembly. Whether a committee is a "standing" or a "special" one, it may be appointed by the presiding officer or elected by the assembly, depending upon the wording of the motion or bylaw authorizing it. Committees should be made up of an odd number of members, with one designated as its permanent chairman, or as a temporary chairman who will convene the committee and preside until a permanent chairman is elected. As with its parent assembly, a majority of a committee's members constitute a quorum.

In any organization there are a number of standing committees—committees appointed to handle special problems throughout a given period of time (a year, the duration of a convention, etc.)—and these committees may make regular reports to the entire membership. Such would be the financial committee, the committee on membership, the public relations committee, and the committee on hospitality.

When there is an occasion for reporting its activities to the entire membership, the chairman of the committee (if a chairman has not been specifically indicated, it is always presumed that the first-named appointee acts as chairman) usually makes the report: *"Mr. Chairman, the Committee on the Budget wishes to report that . . ."* Any action proposed by the committee will ordinarily be stated specifically at the conclusion of the report.

Accepting and Adopting the Committee Report

If the committee's report is one dealing with routine matters, or if it simply wishes to report progress made in its assigned function, there will probably be little desire for discussion by the membership, and the chairman may save time by saying: *"If there is no objection, we will accept* [or *file*] *the report as made."* There being no objections, the chairman will order the secretary to record the acceptance of the report.

If, in addition to reporting its conclusions, the committee also wishes to recommend specific legislation for action it is advisable to do so by introducing appropriate main motions under the heading of new business (see pages 15-26). This procedure has the advantage of permitting the report to be *accepted* or *filed* without the recommended motions being *adopted;* in short, it recognizes the committee report without endorsing it. It also permits the assembly to modify the specific proposals of the committee by amendment, since the committee report itself cannot be amended but must be accepted in whole or in part, or be referred back to the committee with or without specific instructions. The acceptance of a report should be moved by someone other than a committee member. The proposal of motions growing out of the committee's recommendations, however, is customarily made by the committee chairman, although other members may speak in their behalf.

It is assumed that reports of both standing and special committees will be made at the appropriate time in the regular order of business. If this order does not provide for committee reports, or if a committee wishes to report at any other time, it may so inform the chairman of the assembly. He may then direct the committee to submit its report, or he may ask the will of the assembly by putting the undebatable question, requiring a majority vote: *"Shall the report be received at this time?"* If the chairman does not refer the matter to the assembly and any member wishes to object to receiving the report, he may do so and request the chairman to call for a vote. If the assembly votes in the negative, a special time for receiving the report may be set by an appropriate motion or by general consent.

A Minority Committee Report

It may sometimes happen that the point of view of a majority of the members of a committee is vigorously opposed by the remaining members of the committee, and in such cases the minority may also wish to submit a report to the group. After the majority report has been read, a spokesman for the minority may read a separate report, but this report cannot be acted upon unless a motion is made and passed to substitute it for the report of the majority. (See page 20 for the procedure to be followed in making an amendment by substitution.)

The Written Report

In some organizations it is customary for an appointed committee to submit its report in writing to the secretary as well as to make an oral presentation to the whole group. Only the simplest form is necessary for such a written report: *"The Committee on the Budget wishes to report that . . ."* A minority report would read: *"The undersigned, a minority of the Committee on the Budget, . . ."* In either case a written report should include specific statements, in terms of resolutions, if it is felt that some legislative action is necessary. A unanimous report would be signed by the committee chairman and usually by the committee members as well, whereas majority and minority reports would each be signed only by those members supporting them.

D. REPORTS OF SPECIAL COMMITTEES

In addition to the standing committees an organization may have, from time to time, special committees appointed to investigate or consider special matters. Ordinarily the purpose of these committees is to do some of the preliminary work of routine investigation in preparation of a special matter for action by the group as a whole. In almost all respects the handling of a special committee report is identical with the handling of a report of a standing committee, although it must be remembered that ordinarily the business of a special committee is likely to be more controversial than that of a standing committee. In submitting a written report a special committee will vary the form somewhat: *"The committee to which was referred the problem of decreasing membership wishes to report that. . . ."*

E. UNFINISHED BUSINESS

The character of unfinished business is indicated by its descriptive name: it is business which was taken up or considered in a previous meeting but upon which no final action was taken. In the interest of efficiency, therefore, it is taken up in the next meeting before new business is considered. Final action may not have been taken simply because a motion to adjourn was adopted before a decision was reached (since a motion to adjourn takes precedence over all other motions except one), or final action may have been postponed because of a motion made to that effect: *"In order that this assembly may proceed to the more urgent matter of . . . I move that we postpone consideration of the present motion until our next meeting."* In any case, the unfinished business is accorded its proper place in the order of business in the following meeting, at which time final action is taken unless the matter is again delayed by adjournment, postponement, etc. (A more detailed description of the special motions just referred to will be found on pages 32 and 41.)

F. NEW BUSINESS

When business carried over from previous meetings has been disposed of, a group is ready to consider new business. Here, as elsewhere in formal group procedure, efficiency is desired, and to that end it is provided that the group shall consider but one thing at a time, and that each item of business shall be disposed of before another is taken up. In order to facilitate this regular flow of business, organized groups make use of a basic parliamentary device, the motion. A motion is a brief but clear statement of a proposed action to be taken up by the group, and it is the vehicle by which all business is introduced to the group. Because a clear understanding of the use of motions is essential to participation in or conduct of a meeting, that procedure is treated here in some detail.

Introducing Motions

The first step in introducing a motion is to secure recognition from the chairman of the meeting (often referred to as "obtaining the floor"). The member rises and addresses the presiding officer: *"Mr. Chairman."* If the chairman recognizes the speaker, he simply addresses him by name: *"Mr. Doakes."* In a convention or a legislative body the chairman may prefer to say: *"The gentleman from Idaho."* Sometimes several speakers may request recognition at the same time, and then the chairman must decide which one to recognize. This he may do (1) by determining which one addressed him first, (2) by trying to recognize speakers alternately as they are known to him to be for or against a proposal under consideration, or (3) by recognizing a member who has not yet spoken on the question.

When the member receives recognition by the chairman, he "has the floor," or the right to address the assembly, restricted only by such time limits as may have been imposed, or by the interposition of a special motion which has precedence. (See II, "Special Motions.") The usual form for the statement of a motion is: *"I move that. . . ."* It is best to use this simple form even though an arbitrary distinction might be made between motions, resolutions, and other proposals. If, as in some assemblies, it is required that all motions made from the floor also be submitted in writing to the secretary, the same form is used in the written version. Even in the absence of such a rule, the chairman may request that motions be written out for the convenience of the secretary.

Seconding Motions

Before a main motion is thrown open for discussion by the entire group, it must be seconded—that is, some other member of the group must indicate his support of the motion. This he does by saying, even without recognition from the chair, "*I second the motion.*" The obvious purpose of requiring a second is to determine that at least two members are interested in a certain proposal before it is allowed to occupy the attention of the whole group. It is essential that there be a second, but it is not necessary that the seconder be identified by the chairman, or that his name be recorded in the minutes by the secretary. If no second is made to a motion, the chairman may ask: "*Is there a second to the motion?*" Hearing one, he will say: "*The motion is seconded.*" Or, hearing none, he may say: "*The motion is not seconded,*" or "*The motion is lost for want of a second.*" In such event the meeting is again open for another original motion.

Not all motions, it should be noted, require a second. As will be observed later, a call for the orders of the day, a point of order, or an objection to the consideration of a question, may be considered without a second. Often a routine matter of business (where unanimity is a foregone conclusion) is also acted upon without a second. In nominations for office no second is necessary, although particularly in nominating conventions it is customary to make seconds to nominations simply to "get on the record."

Discussing Motions

When a motion has been made and seconded, the chairman is then ready to state the motion and to open it for discussion. He may simply say: "*You have heard the motion, which has been seconded. Is there any discussion?*" Or, if the motion is long or complex, he may either repeat it himself or call upon the secretary to read it, and then call for discussion.

If it should occur to the chairman, the maker of the motion, or any member of the group that a change should be made in the phrasing of the original motion in the interest of clarity or accuracy, such a change may be suggested. With the approval of the maker of the motion this change may be incorporated in the chairman's formal statement. The approval of a change in statement by the member who seconded the original motion is not necessary, although the chairman must be sure that some member seconds the rephrased motion.

Once the motion has been thus formally stated by the chairman, and provided it is a debatable motion (see II, "Special Motions"), it is open for discussion (limited only by such time limits as the group may have adopted). At this point the phrasing of the motion cannot be changed (except by amendment), nor can even the maker of the motion withdraw it (except by unanimous consent to his request, or by a majority vote if he moves permission), for it is considered "in the possession of the assembly."

During the discussion the same general rules as were described above (see "Introducing Motions") will govern the chairman in his recognition of members of the group. Once a member of the group obtains the floor, it is his until he finishes speaking (or until any time limit on remarks has expired). There are certain special motions (see II, "Special Motions") which may interrupt him, but when they have been disposed of, he may resume his speaking. If another member wishes to ask a question of the speaker, he may address the chairman, and the chairman will ask the speaker to "yield" long enough to hear the question and reply to it, but the speaker is not obligated to do so. (See page 40.)

Amending Motions

When the chairman has made a formal statement of a motion to the group and it is open for discussion, members may wish to suggest specific changes in the text of the motion, and to do this they make use of the parliamentary device called an amendment. An amendment may be defined as a formal proposal for a change in a main motion; when it is stated, it needs a second, and it is then before the group for discussion as would be any other debatable motion. (An amendment is debatable when it is applied to a debatable motion. See II, "Special Motions.")

An amendment to a main motion may ordinarily be made in any of four forms: elimination, addition, substitution, or division. To understand each of these procedures let us assume that this main motion has been submitted to a group assembly: *"I move that this organization go on record as supporting the taxation and foreign policy programs of the present administration."*

Elimination: A member who feels that he can support the tax program but not the foreign policy program may formally suggest the elimination of that feature of the motion by saying: *"I move that the motion be amended by striking out [eliminating] the words* AND FOREIGN POLICY.*"*

Addition: Another member may feel that the farm program of the administration should also be supported by the group, and so he may say: *"I move that the motion be amended by inserting [adding], after the word* POLICY, *the words* AND FARM.*"*

Substitution: A third member may prefer the term *national defense* because it is more comprehensive than *foreign policy,* so he says: *"I move that the motion be amended by substituting*

the words NATIONAL DEFENSE *in place of the words* FOREIGN
POLICY."

It is also permissible to move to substitute an entirely new
motion, instead of merely changing a few words in the pending
one. This is a desirable procedure when an assembly would
otherwise require a number of detailed amendments to make the
original motion acceptable. Such a proposal is referred to as a
"substitute motion," rather than "a motion to amend by substitution," and can be put this way: *"I move to substitute for the
present motion the following motion. . . ."*

Division: Finally, there may be a member who feels that it
will be unfortunate if the two aspects of the administration's
program are considered together, and so may wish to separate
the two features of the main motion for separate discussion and
vote. He may then say: *"I move that the motion be divided and
that this body consider first the taxation program and then the
foreign policy program."* Or, more simply: *"I call for* [request]
a division of the question." If there are no objections, the chairman may divide the question without an approving vote.

Following any one of these procedures, a member of the
group may amend any main motion which is amendable, although it is preferable that no amendment simply negate (as by
substituting "that we do" for "that we do not"), even though it
is hostile to the object of the original motion or to the method
proposed for achieving that object. Obviously if an amendment
simply reverses the intent of the original motion from affirmative to negative, the same result can be achieved more simply
by defeating the original motion.

Another rule is that an amendment to a main motion (often
called a first-degree amendment) may itself be amended but
once (by a second-degree amendment); that is, there can be a
main motion, and an amendment to the main motion, and an

amendment to the amendment. To permit further amending of amendments would lead only to confusion. It is possible, however, to make any number of first-degree amendments. The only limiting rule is that each one must be disposed of before another is introduced.

When a bill has been presented to a legislative conference or a convention, there may be a number of amendments to specific sections or paragraphs. In this event the amendments should be taken up in the order in which they apply to the bill: amendments to the first section first, and so on. A long and complicated bill may always be considered by sections (*seriatim*), rather than as a whole (*in toto*), at the request of a member if there are no objections, or upon the adoption of a motion to that effect. When this is done, individual sections are perfected by amendment but not voted on separately; a final vote to adopt the entire measure is taken only after considering each section.

A final rule to be observed is the common-sense one that all amendments must be germane or relevant to the original motion. The chair is empowered to rule out of order any amendment he considers irrelevant, although his decision may be appealed from (see page 39).

It must be remembered that the order of precedence in considering amendments is clear: first the amendment to the amendment, then the amendment, and finally the main motion. Only discussion pertaining to the pending question (the amendment or main motion under consideration) is permitted, and each question must be disposed of by adoption or rejection before the next one may be considered. It should be noted that the adoption of an amendment may give no indication of the final disposal of the main motion, for it is possible that several amendments may be approved, but the main motion rejected. In such a case the adopted amendments are officially dead.

Voting on Motions

After the discussion upon a given motion seems to have been concluded, the chairman may say: *"Are you ready for the question?"* If this query evokes a general chorus of *"Question!"* or if no one else rises to speak, the chairman will conclude consideration of the motion by "putting the question." If the response is mixed, however, the chairman must exercise his discretion in proceeding to a vote, neither arbitrarily insisting upon a vote when legitimate discussion is not yet concluded, nor permitting unnecessary delay by frivolous, irrelevant, or repetitious discussion. If any member wishes to continue serious discussion, however, he must be permitted to do so. Only when a two-thirds majority wishes to vote immediately or to limit debate (see pages 29–31) can discussion formally be terminated. It may sometimes happen that a member of the group will call *"Question!"* thus urging the chairman to put the pending motion to an immediate vote. In such cases the chairman must be sure that this single member's demand represents the sentiment of the whole group. When the chairman "puts the question," he repeats the motion (as he did before the discussion began), or, if it is long and detailed, he asks the secretary to read it. If he states the motion, he simply says: *"The question is whether this body wishes to adopt the motion that . . ."*

After the question has been stated, the chairman may say: *"You have heard the motion. All those in favor will say aye* [pause]; *those opposed will say no* [pause]. *The motion is carried* [or *lost*]." When the feeling is nearly unanimous, such a vocal vote will suffice; when there is a more nearly balanced division of opinion, the chairman may, instead, ask that there be a "show of hands" or that members rise in their places. In some organizations, on the other hand, it may be provided that there be a roll-call vote, or that the vote be taken by ballot.

If any member is in doubt as to the correctness of the chairman's decision after a voice has been taken, however, he may call for a division of the assembly to give a more accurate count. (*"Mr. Chairman, I call for a show of hands on the motion."*) The chairman is obliged to grant his request.

In any event the chairman must specifically call for an affirmative and a negative vote and announce the result before the motion can be considered as officially adopted or rejected.

It may happen that the votes for adoption and the votes for rejection are equal in number. In such a case the chairman may break the tie by casting his own vote either way, provided he is also a member of the organization over which he presides. This he may do publicly, or he may privately inform the secretary of his own choice, and then announce the final vote without specifying that he voted one way or the other. If the chairman does not wish to vote, the tie will, of course, result in the rejection of the motion, inasmuch as a simple majority (one more than half of those voting) is ordinarily required for passage. The chairman may also cast a vote at any other time when his vote will change the result. Thus, if a motion lacked one vote of being defeated, the chairman could cast a negative vote and cause the motion to be defeated by a tie vote.

Unless the standing rules of the organization provide otherwise, it is always assumed that the majority requirement applies to those voting and not to those present. Thus a motion might be carried by the votes of a majority of those voting, even though those voting were a minority of those present. This practice is based upon the assumption that those who do not vote are neutral or indifferent toward the matter at hand. This same assumption applies to those members of an organization who do not attend a meeting—if they are not present, they are presumed not to have any great interest in the problem under consideration and therefore acquiescent to the decision of those who do attend the meeting.

It may occasionally happen that a member wishes to change his vote from "aye" to "no," or vice versa, after making an initial decision; this is especially true in a convention when a minority delegation wishes to "get aboard the bandwagon." In such cases a change in the vote is ordinarily permitted so long as the final result of the voting has not been announced. Once the final tally has been announced, the motion is officially disposed of and no changes may be made—except that special parliamentary action may be taken to "reconsider." (See page 36.)

It should also be noted that a special parliamentary practice is to permit a member to rise belatedly for discussion of a motion, even during the voting upon it, up until the time that the negative vote is called for. The obvious purpose is to provide even the most timid or reticent member with a last-minute opportunity to make his point. Once the negative vote is called for, no further discussion is in order, but if discussion is resumed before that point, the previously taken affirmative vote is canceled and the motion is again before the house.

The chairman must always announce whether a motion was passed or defeated; after a division of the assembly he also reports the number of "yeas" and "nays." He can easily calculate whether a motion requiring a two-thirds majority has been carried by multiplying the negative vote by two. If the product is equal to or less than the affirmative vote, the motion has carried by a two-thirds majority.

Procedures in Elections

The nominating and electing of officers is ordinarily considered "new business." The exact procedures to be followed are usually set forth in the bylaws of an organization. If they are not, the matter becomes a proper subject for a main motion at the appropriate time. This motion may prescribe a sequence of steps to be followed and is introduced, debated, and voted upon as any other main motion. In more formal and permanent groups it is usually provided that nominations be made by a nominating, or "slate," committee. At the proper time this committee places the persons it has selected in nomination. The chairman then asks if there are other nominations to be made from the floor; if there are any, they have the same status as those submitted by the committee. In more informal groups the chairman may simply announce, at the proper time: *"Nominations are now open for president . . . secretary . . . etc."* Any member wishing to place the name of another member in nomination says: *"I nominate John Doakes for president."* A second is not necessary.

Whatever the procedure followed in making the nominations, a common practice prevails in closing them. If it is apparent that all nominations have been made, the chairman may declare the nominations closed, or any member may initiate this action with a special motion to that effect: *"I move that the nominations be closed."* This motion must be seconded, but it cannot be debated; and it requires a two-thirds majority vote for adoption. It may be amended only to provide a specific time for closing the nominations. When this motion is adopted, the election vote may be taken by any of the several procedures already outlined, though voting by ballot is preferable in elections. If the vote is not taken by ballot, but by a show of hands, the candidates' names should be presented for voting in the order in which they were nominated.

In some organizations it is customary to ask those nominated to leave the room during the vote in order to avoid possible embarrassment. Since this procedure means that candidates lose the right to vote, it argues for the use of the secret ballot. Usually a committee of tellers is appointed to count the ballots, and also to enforce whatever regulations may govern the method of marking ballots validly. The bylaws, of course, may provide a special method of voting for officers. Ordinarily a plurality (more votes than any other candidate) is sufficient for election, although the bylaws may provide special procedures for securing an election by a majority.

G. MISCELLANEOUS

The next to the last item in the accepted order of business provides for the consideration of any matters which do not properly fall within the subject matter of the preceding items. At this point the chairman may ask if there are any *"announcements, requests, or items,"* none of which would ordinarily require definite action. In a convention program this place in the order of business may be the most appropriate for passing general or customary resolutions in appreciation of the services of the hospitality or arrangements committee, and so on.

H. ADJOURNMENT

It may sometimes be provided in standing rules that a meeting be regularly adjourned at a specific time, or a main motion may have been adopted at the outset of a meeting to adjourn at a stated time. In such cases, when the fixed time has arrived, the chairman may simply say: *"The hour fixed for adjournment has been reached, and the meeting is now declared adjourned."* Ordinarily, however, he may call for a vote on a pending motion before adjourning the meeting if it is apparent that the members are willing.

When no special provision has been made for a time at which to adjourn, the matter is decided by action upon a regular motion to that effect. Three special rules apply to the motion for adjournment: (1) it may not interrupt a speaker or the process of voting on a motion; (2) it is not debatable; (3) it may not be amended. If properly made and seconded, the motion to adjourn must be put to an immediate vote of the assembly. The motion may be interrupted, however, by a privileged motion whose purpose is to fix the time for reassembling. Such a motion may be amended, and, though the main motion may not be debated, the amendment may be.

If the motion to adjourn is adopted, the chairman simply announces the result of the voting and declares the meeting adjourned. If the motion is defeated, the regular order of business is resumed. It is possible that shortly thereafter still another motion to adjourn may be proposed, and the discretion of the chairman must be exercised to determine whether the situation has changed sufficiently to permit the motion to occupy the time of the group. That is, if the chairman feels that the group clearly expressed a desire to conclude a given matter of business by its earlier refusal to adjourn, he may simply not entertain the renewed motion.

Recess

A motion to adjourn should not be confused with a motion to recess. If for any special reason a recess is thought desirable (to permit tabulation of votes, a party caucus, or simply a brief respite), a motion to recess may interrupt any other business (but not a speaker). The usual form of such a motion is: *"I move that we declare a recess for fifteen minutes."* This may be amended (to change the length of the recess), and the amendment may be debated, although the main motion may not be If a motion to recess for a given period of time is adopted, the chairman declares the recess and then calls the meeting to order again at the expiration of the recess period.

II

SPECIAL MOTIONS

As has been indicated earlier, the conduct of formal group meetings often requires the use of special parliamentary motions to meet particular types of situation. Many of them will be employed only rarely, and others are used more commonly, but an acquaintance with all of them is helpful in furthering democratic and efficient conduct of business. Since these motions are special ones, they differ in several important ways from the usual main motion and its related amendments.

1. The form in which they are presented and their phraseology are ordinarily fixed and more or less standardized because they represent special ways of dealing with main motions. For this reason, also, many of them may not be amended.

2. Because some of them are especially designed to treat of main motions in special ways, they are in order when main motions are being discussed, and some of them may also be in order even when they interrupt a speaker who has the floor.

3. Their special character makes them relate to rather than replace a main motion, and hence they are disposed of as rapidly as possible. This means, in many cases, that special motions are not debatable.

4. In the case of certain special motions the action which they propose is drastic, and they therefore require an unusual majority of two thirds in order to be adopted.

Not all these special features pertain to any given special motion; when any of them do apply, that fact will be especially noted in the discussion which follows. In all other cases it should be assumed that the special motion is governed only by the principles already discussed in connection with ordinary main motions.

To make a study of these special motions both functional and practical, we have grouped them under separate headings according to their purposes: (*a*) to suppress debate or hasten action; (*b*) to delay action; (*c*) to prevent action; (*d*) to consider more carefully; (*e*) to change a decision; (*f*) to maintain rules and order; (*g*) to close a meeting. Sometimes a special motion may serve several of these purposes, but it commonly serves only one.

The paragraphs which follow will each deal with one of these special motions, numbered consecutively to correspond with their position on the chart of special motions classified according to purpose (see the back cover). A brief study of the special character, limitations, and application of each one should make the chart alone an adequate reference during an actual meeting.

A. TO SUPPRESS DEBATE OR HASTEN ACTION

1. Previous Question (or Vote Immediately)

The purpose of this special motion is to terminate discussion of any debatable motion by bringing it to an immediate vote. It is neither amendable nor debatable and requires a two-thirds majority for adoption. If it is adopted, the previous question (the main motion to which it was applied) must be voted upon without further debate. If it is rejected, the debate continues on the main motion as though the previous question had not been moved. The traditional form for this motion is: *"Mr. Chairman, I move the previous [pending] question."* Or the member may say: *"Mr. Chairman, I move that we vote immediately upon the motion now before the house."* The chairman will put the motion by saying: *"The motion is for an immediate vote upon the pending question . . ."* or *"It has been moved that we vote immediately and without further discussion upon the question before us. . . ."*

2. Suspend Rules

The purpose of this motion is to make possible for a temporary period a procedure which is contrary to the standing rules or the rules of order, such as the consideration of a motion that would otherwise be out of order. The motion to suspend the rules is neither debatable nor amendable and requires a two-thirds majority for adoption. If adopted, the suspension is in force only as long as consideration is being given to the motion for which the rules were suspended; after it has been disposed of, the rules are again in force. A member might make this motion by saying: *"Mr. Chairman, I move to suspend the rules in order to . . ."* (state specific purpose).

3. Limit Debate

The purpose of this motion is to restrict the time available for debate in order to expedite business, and it usually has the effect of limiting debate only upon the pending motion or amendment. It may, however, be adopted to apply to a whole meeting, regardless of what questions may arise. In any case the motion should specify the desired limitations: of the time for the whole discussion of a motion, of the number of speakers favoring and opposing it, of the length of speeches on it, and so on. The motion to limit debate is not debatable, and it requires a two-thirds majority for adoption. The usual form for this motion is: *"Mr. Chairman, I move to limit debate on the pending question* [or *on all questions*] *to . . ."* (state limit). It should be noted that a converse motion is also possible, extending a previously imposed limit on debate.

4. Take from the Table (or Resume Consideration)

The purpose of this motion is to take from the table, or revive, a motion which some time previously has been disposed of by being laid on the table, or temporarily put aside. The motion to take from the table has the status of a new motion and thus cannot interrupt other business. It is neither amendable nor debatable, and requires a simple majority for adoption. If it is adopted, the motion taken from the table becomes the next order of business. If it is rejected, the order of business remains unchanged, although the motion to take from the table may be renewed at a later time within the same session of meetings. A member makes the motion by saying: *"Mr. Chairman, I move to take from the table the motion to . . ."* or, more informally, *"I move that we resume discussion of the motion to. . . ."*

5. Make Special Order of Business

The purpose of this motion is to set a specific time for the exclusive consideration of a particular question. It differs from most other special motions in that it requires a two-thirds majority vote for its adoption; the propriety of its application to any particular question is a subject for amendment and debate. If the motion is adopted, the stated item becomes a special matter of business at the specified time; if it is rejected, the normal order of business is followed. A member introduces it by saying: *"Mr. Chairman, I move that the matter of . . . be made a special order of business to be considered . . ."* (state specific time). When the specified time arrives, the chairman must interrupt pending business to submit the special order. If he fails to do so, any member may interrupt pending business or even a speaker to call for the special order. The call requires no second, is neither debatable nor amendable, and must be put to an immediate vote by the chairman. An affirmative vote on the call leaves pending business unfinished; a negative vote temporarily postpones the special order until the pending business is disposed of.

B. TO DELAY ACTION

6. Postpone to a Certain Time (or Postpone Definitely)

The purpose of this motion is to delay until a specified time any action upon a pending question. It may be both amended and debated and requires a simple majority for adoption. If it is adopted, the main motion to which it is applied is laid aside until the time specified; if it is rejected, the main motion remains the current business of the meeting. The usual form is: *"Mr. Chairman, I move that consideration of the pending question be postponed until . . ."* (state specific time). It should be noted that this motion, and either of the other two motions designed to delay action, applies to all pending questions whether so stated or not. That is, if introduced when a main motion is on the floor, it applies also to amendments to that motion; if introduced when an amendment is on the floor, it applies also to the main motion whose amendment is being considered.

7. Lay on the Table (or Postpone Temporarily)

The purpose of this motion is to postpone consideration of a subject by laying it on the table, figuratively, from which it may be taken up again at some later time in the same session or at any subsequent session. (See above, 4, "Take from the table.") If it is assumed that a majority cannot be mustered to take it up from the table during the current session, the purpose may be to stop debate and to suppress the question for the remainder of the session, or even to defeat it permanently. The motion may be applied to any pending main motion but may not interrupt a speaker. It is neither amendable nor debatable. One may make it by saying: *"Mr. Chairman, I move to lay on the table the pending motion to. . . ."*

8. Refer to Committee (or Commit)

The purpose of referring a motion to a committee may be simply to delay action upon it or to obtain the advantages of more careful investigation and discussion by a smaller group. The motion may be amended to name the committee, set a time for its report, and so on, and may be debated. It may be applied to any pending main motion. The usual statement is: *"Mr. Chairman, I move to refer the matter of . . . to a committee . . ."* (specify if desired).

C. TO PREVENT ACTION

9. Object to Consideration

The purpose of this action is to object to the consideration of a specific question which the maker feels the group should not discuss, because of its irrelevance, frivolousness, objectionable nature, and so on. It is unusual in that it does not need a second, and that it may interrupt a speaker. It is neither amendable nor debatable, and it requires a two-thirds majority vote. The chairman may, on his own initiative, object to consideration of a specific question and put the matter to a vote. If adopted, the objection has the effect of suppressing the question; if rejected, it has no effect upon the pending question. In some cases the chairman may make a ruling on the objection without putting it to a vote, but an appeal may always be made from that ruling (see below, 17, "Appeal from decision of chair.") He may say: *"The chair sustains the member's objection and rules the question now being considered out of order."* If he wishes to put the objection to a vote, he says: *"An objection has been raised to the consideration of the question now up for discussion. Those in favor of considering the question. . . . Those opposed to considering the question. . . ."* The objection itself is usually presented in this form: *"Mr. Chairman, I object to the consideration of the question of. . . ."* The objector may or may not state his reasons, but his objection to any main motion can be made only before there has been any debate upon it.

10. Withdraw a Motion

The purpose of this motion is to prevent action upon a motion when the maker has changed his mind about it, when he is persuaded to withdraw the motion in order to expedite other and more urgent business. Ordinarily the request need not be seconded; the chairman will simply ask: *"Is there any objection to the withdrawal of Mr. Doakes' motion?"* If there is none, the motion is withdrawn automatically. The seconder of the original motion need not be especially consulted, for every member has an opportunity to object to the withdrawal of the motion if he wishes. If there is any objection, the chairman may put the matter to a vote without the formality of a special and seconded motion. The request may be neither amended nor debated; and, though it may be made when the original motion is being debated, it may not interrupt a speaker. If the request is adopted, the original motion is as if it had never been made;

if the request is rejected, discussion of the original motion continues. The request may best be stated in this form: "*Mr. Chairman, I ask permission to withdraw my motion to. . . .*" Should this request fail to gain unanimous consent the chairman takes a vote by saying: "*Mr. Doakes has asked permission to withdraw his motion. Those in favor of granting his request. . . . Those opposed to granting his request. . . .*"

11. Postpone Indefinitely

The purpose of the motion to postpone indefinitely is to dispose of a question without voting upon it, or perhaps to test voting strength on the question without actually voting upon it. The motion may not be amended but may be debated. If adopted, it has the effect of postponing the question until some future session, when it must be reintroduced as a completely new motion, and thus the effect is to kill the motion without voting upon it directly. If the motion to postpone is rejected, the question to which it was applied remains current. The form of the motion may be: "*Mr. Chairman, I move that consideration of the motion to . . . be indefinitely postponed.*"

D. TO CONSIDER MORE CAREFULLY

12. Committee of the Whole (or Consider Informally)

The purpose of this motion is to apply to a specific question the more informal methods of small group discussion in a meeting of all of the members of a group, and it is used for such questions as merit the careful committeelike study of all the members. The only motions in order in committee of the whole are to amend, adopt, "rise and report" to the assembly, and appeals from the chair's decisions. Debate is unlimited unless restricted in the original motion to go into committee of the whole.

It is unusual in that it may interrupt the consideration of the problem under discussion. It is both amendable and debatable. If adopted, it resolves the assembly into a committe of the whole, and the chairman usually appoints some other member to preside and also a temporary secretary. If rejected, it has no effect upon the discussion of the question to which it was applied. The form of the motion may be: *"Mr. Chairman, I move that this body go into a committee of the whole for the purpose of considering. . . ."* or *"Mr. Chairman, I move that we consider informally the matter of. . . ."* If the motion carries, the assembly turns immediately to the matter referred to the committee of the whole or to be considered informally; as soon as this matter is disposed of, the assembly returns to its normal status and procedure. In legislative bodies the presiding officer relinquishes the chair to some other member when in the committee of the whole, but in most clubs and associations the presiding officer commonly continues his functions.

E. TO CHANGE A DECISION

13. Reconsider

The purpose of the motion to reconsider is to give an assembly an opportunity to consider again an action already taken. It may be applied to actions other than a recess, an adjournment, a suspension of rules, or a motion to reconsider. It may not be amended and may be debated only if the original motion for which reconsideration is moved was debatable. Because the motion to reconsider would always result in upholding the original decision if no member changed his mind, the motion is governed by a special rule that the motion to reconsider must be made by a person who was on the prevailing side in the original voting. Thus a change of at least one vote is indicated.

(In some organizations this special requirement is waived on the grounds that if the original vote was a voice vote, the position of any one individual cannot be determined. Although this waiver of the traditional rule is increasingly common, organizations following Robert's *Rules of Order, Revised,* must adhere to it.) A second special rule is that the motion to reconsider must be made at the same meeting or at the next meeting following the original vote. The motion may interrupt a speaker, but the pending business must be disposed of before the motion to reconsider can be taken up. If the motion to reconsider is adopted, its effect is to resume debate on the original motion as though it had not been disposed of. If rejected, the motion to reconsider has no effect on the status of the original motion. (A common-sense limitation on this motion, of course, is that if irrevocable actions have been taken in consequence of adopting the original motion—such as signing contracts or paying money—it is too late to reconsider.) The form for putting this motion is: *"Mr. Chairman, I move to reconsider the action of this assembly in. . . ."* Under traditional rules the chairman must then ask the member: *"Did you vote on the prevailing side?"* or, if the original vote was by roll call, he may consult the secretary's records on the point. Only when the response to this question is affirmative may the chairman accept the motion to reconsider. (Under more liberal rules, the chairmen accepts the motion without question.)

14. Rescind

The purpose of the motion to rescind is to cancel an action taken at a previous meeting. The motion is both amendable and debatable, but it may not interrupt other business. If it is adopted, the previously taken action is made of no effect; if it is rejected, the previously taken action is not affected. This motion to rescind is occasionally amended to expunge (officially delete, normally by drawing a line through this point of the secretary's minutes) the reference to the previous action. In form the motion may be: *"Mr. Chairman, I move to rescind the action of . . . taken at the . . . meeting."* If the motion to rescind has been announced in a previous meeting, or in the call for a meeting, only a simple majority is needed to pass it; otherwise it requires a two-thirds majority. Unlike the motion to reconsider, the motion to rescind may be introduced by one who did not vote on the prevailing side in the original voting.

F. TO MAINTAIN RULES AND ORDER

15. Question of Privilege

The purpose of this action is to request the chairman to deal with emergency situations, disorders, personal and offending remarks, or other circumstances affecting the comfort or welfare of the members. It is unusual, for it needs no second, and it may interrupt business or a speaker. It is neither amendable nor debatable. A decision on the question may be rendered by the chairman (from which the maker may appeal—see below, 17, "Appeal from decision of the chair"), or the chairman may submit the matter to the assembly for a vote. If the question of privilege is upheld, the chairman will grant the member's request and take appropriate action; if the question is denied, no personal privilege is deemed to have been violated. The usual form for this action is: *"Mr. Chairman, I rise to a question of personal privilege."* The chairman will then ask the member to state his question of privilege, following which the chairman will either make his ruling or submit the question to a general vote. In the latter case the chairman may say: *"The chairman is in some doubt as to the question of privilege raised by the mem-*

ber and refers the matter to the assembly for decision. The question is whether. . . . Those who believe it is. . . . Those who believe it is not. . . ."

16. Point of Order

The purpose of this motion is to correct an error in procedure or in following the order of business. It may be raised whenever a member feels that debate on a given question is out of order, that another member's remarks are irrelevant, and so on. Like the question of privilege, it needs no second, and it may interrupt a speaker. It is neither amendable nor debatable. Ordinarily it will be put as: *"Mr. Chairman, I rise to a point of order."* The chairman will request the member to state his point of order, and the chairman will then give a ruling on the point, or he may submit the question to a vote. If the objection is upheld by the chairman, or by the assembly, the procedure is corrected. If the objection is denied, the discussion or point in question is not affected. If the point of order is decided by the chairman and any member feels dissatisfied, he may appeal from the decision of the chair (see below, 17, "Appeal from decision of chair").

17. Appeal from Decision of Chair

The purpose of this motion is to appeal to the assembly to override a ruling made by the chairman. It must be seconded and must be made immediately after the chairman's ruling. It may not be amended but may be debated unless it relates to an undebatable question, priority of business, or indecorum. The chairman may participate in the debate to the extent of explaining or defending his original decision, and at the conclusion of the debate he may reply to any arguments made against his decision. When the motion is put to a vote, the question is upon sustaining the chairman's decision. The usual form of the motion is: "*Mr. Chairman, I appeal from the decision of the chair.*" After the appeal has been seconded, the chairman says: "*The decision of the chair has been appealed from. The question is upon sustaining that decision. Those in favor of sustaining the decision of the chair. . . . Those opposed to sustaining the decision of the chair. . . .*" Either a majority or a tie vote has the effect of sustaining the decision of the chairman.

18. Parliamentary Inquiry

The purpose of this action is to enable any member of an assembly to seek advice from the chairman concerning the proper parliamentary procedure to be followed in making an appropriate motion or in rising to a point of order in connection with a pending matter of business. Thus a member who wishes to propose action but who is not sure how to do so properly may obtain information from the chairman, who is presumably well informed as to appropriate procedures. Like other special actions designed to maintain rules and order, the parliamentary inquiry may interrupt a speaker. The simplest form of statement is: "*Mr. Chairman, I rise to a parliamentary inquiry.*" The chairman will then ask the member to state his question. If an immediate response is necessary, the chairman will give it; otherwise he may reserve his reply until the speaker who has the floor has concluded. No second is needed for a parliamentary inquiry, and it is not amendable or debatable.

19. Request for Information

The purpose of this action is similar to that of the parliamentary inquiry. Specifically, it is designed to permit any member of an assembly to request information concerning pending business either from the chairman or from a speaker who has the floor. It may, therefore, interrupt a speaker. If the request for information can be answered by the chairman, the member rises and says: *"Mr. Chairman, I rise for information."* The chairman may then give the desired information or, if the question is not urgent, may delay the response until after the speaker who has the floor has concluded his remarks. If the member's request for information is directed to the speaker then holding the floor, he will say: *"Mr. Chairman, I should like to ask the gentleman a question."* To this request the chairman responds by asking the speaker: *"Will the gentleman yield for a question?"* If the speaker accedes to this request, which he is not obliged to do, the chairman then invites the questioner to put his question. In a formal assembly it is usually assumed that members will not speak directly to each other; therefore the questioner asks his question through the chairman: *"Mr. Chairman, I should like to ask the gentleman. . . ."* The speaker will direct his reply to the chairman in the same way. (In an assembly operating informally, members do address each other, directly but courteously, although never without first being recognized by the chairman.) A request for information needs no second, and is not an action which may be debated or amended.

G. TO CLOSE A MEETING

20. Adjourn

The purpose of the motion to adjourn is to close the meeting, or perhaps, at times, to terminate consideration of a question. The motion may not interrupt a speaker but is in order at any time. It is neither amendable nor debatable, and must be put to an immediate vote by the chairman. If it is adopted, the meeting is adjourned upon the chairman's declaration, although he may withhold such declaration to permit time for a special motion to fix the time at which to reassemble (see below, 21, "Fix time of next meeting"). If the motion is rejected, the pending business is continued. The simplest form is: *"Mr. Chairman, I move that we adjourn."*

21. Fix Time of Next Meeting

The purpose of this motion is to fix a time (or place) for re-assembling. The motion may be amended to substitute a different time, and such an amendment may be debated although the main motion is not debatable. The motion to fix a time for the next meeting may be in order even after the passage of a motion to adjourn if the chairman has not declared final adjournment. Often the fixing of a time to meet again is incorporated with the motion of adjournment of the current meeting. If adopted, the motion governs the time of reassembling; if it is rejected, the time of the next meeting will be governed by the standing rules or the bylaws. The motion may be stated: *"Mr. Chairman, I move that the time of the next meeting be. . . ."*

22. Recess

The purpose of the motion to recess is temporarily to disband the meeting to provide a respite from business, the counting of votes, strengthening of party lines, securing additional information and so on. The motion may not interrupt a speaker, but it may interrupt any business other than the actual procedure of voting. It may be amended to alter the length of the proposed recess, and such amendment may be debated although the main motion may not be. If adopted, the motion has the effect of declaring the stipulated recess; if rejected, it has no effect upon the pending business. The simplest form of statement is: *"Mr. Chairman, I move a recess for . . ."* (specify time).

III

PRECEDENCE OF MOTIONS

Throughout the preceding discussion of the nature and application of special motions it has no doubt been apparent that some ranking of these motions according to precedence is an essential of parliamentary procedure. Without some means of determining the relative rank of motions competing for the attention of an assembly unnecessarily complex and even incongruous situations would often arise. The law of usage has determined the order of precedence indicated by the following list, and careful adherence to it will facilitate fair and efficient action in the everyday business meeting. The precedence of a motion determines whether it may be considered in any given circumstance or must be ruled out of order. If the proposed motion ranks higher on the precedence list than the motion under discussion, it takes precedence: the chairman must accept it and it must be disposed of at once. If the proposed motion ranks lower, it has no precedence, is out of order, and the chairman cannot accept it. (For a complete chart of motions classified according to precedence, see inside the back cover.)

Privileged Motions

These have precedence over all others since they are related to the welfare of the group as a whole rather than to any particular motion before the group. In the order of their precedence among themselves they are:

> Fix time of next meeting
> Adjourn
> Recess
> Question of privilege

Subsidiary Motions

These yield precedence to the privileged motions and take precedence over main motions. Because subsidiary motions are concerned with the disposal or modification of a main motion, they must be disposed of before the main motion to which they apply. In the order of their precedence among themselves they are:

> Lay on the table (or postpone temporarily)
> Previous question (or vote immediately)
> Limit debate
> Postpone to a certain time (or postpone definitely)
> Refer to committee (or commit)
> Committee of the whole (or consider informally)
> Amend
> Postpone indefinitely

Main Motions

These are of the lowest rank and have precedence over no others, inasmuch as they provide the vehicles which introduce all new business into an assembly. Without regard to any order of precedence among themselves they are:

> Main motion for general business
> Take from the table (or resume consideration)
> Reconsider

Rescind

Make special order of business

Incidental Motions

These motions do not properly fall within the list of precedence since they usually arise out of business before the assembly, may be proposed at any time, and must be decided as they arise. They do, of course, take precedence over motions to which they are incidental, and thus rank as a group between subsidiary and privileged motions. Without precedence among themselves they are:

Point of order

Appeal from decision of chair

Suspend rules

Object to consideration

Parliamentary inquiry

Request for information

Withdraw a motion

IV

DUTIES OF THE
PRESIDING OFFICER

By custom and constitutional provision the president of an organization presides over its business meetings, with the vice-president presiding in the president's absence. Throughout this manual we have noted specific duties of the presiding officer; here we consider his role in somewhat broader terms and summarize his duties before, during, and after meetings.

Although each member of an organization bears a responsibility for its successful operation, the presiding officer's role is a major one in the business meeting. Essentially he is an agent of his group: he has a fixed responsibility, not just for presiding over whatever discussion may happen to take place, but for seeing to it that enough relevant discussion takes places to carry out the proper business of the meeting. He cannot be as casual in his approach as if he were leading an informal discussion; he cannot be as innocent of a prepared agenda, either. If the business at hand, for example, is the annual election of new officers, the chairman as agent of the organization is responsible not just for having the assembly "talk it over," or "discuss the problem," but for getting new officers expeditiously nominated and fairly elected.

To carry out his duties effectively the chairman needs special qualifications:

He needs rapport with the members of his organization. He must know and understand them; they must have confidence in his fairness and respect for his firmness. "Goodtime Charlie" may be handy at a party, but a good chairman cannot be too eager to please everyone. "Caspar Milquetoast" may have quiet qualities, but chairmanship often requires vigorous and resolute leadership. And "Nervous Nellie" is about as useful in the chairman's seat as she is in the back seat of your automobile.

He needs a solid knowledge of parliamentary procedure. If ignorance is ever bliss, it certainly is not so in the case of a presiding officer. He must have the same precise knowledge of form and procedure as the hostess at a formal dinner, not because the form is an end in itself, but because it contributes to smooth and efficient operation. The presiding officer needs to understand the philosophy and objects of parliamentary procedure (maintaining order, expediting business, and ensuring equality of opportunity in decision-making), as well as the technical means (order of business, formal motions, and standard procedures), by which these objectives are accomplished.

He needs positive personal attributes. In physical terms, he must be able to speak up and make himself heard. Intellectually he must have the capacity for making quick decisions, analyzing the parliamentary situation, and applying appropriate procedures. Sometimes he may be provided with a parliamentarian, but if he must consult this authority constantly before rendering decisions, he had better trade places and let the man who knows wield the gavel. Most important are the chairman's psychological attributes, his sensitivity to people, his awareness not only of what members are saying from the floor, but how they feel about what they say. *Judgment, common sense, tact,* and *impartiality* are the virtue words that apply, but they do not completely describe the chairman's need for being able to sense the mood of the group or the attitude of its members. Like the jockey in a horse race, the chairman must know when to relax and when to apply the pressure.

Though the presiding officer possesses these qualifications, his role will be affected by certain variables: the size of the group, its knowledge of parliamentary procedure, and the division of its opinions. The chairman must take these factors as he finds them, and weigh them in determining whether his rule shall be more formal, rather than less. Even this generalization must be modified by the extent to which members of his organization are acquainted with and used to working with each other. Though he is guided by standard rules, the presiding officer must often "play by ear" as he plans, conducts, and evaluates the meeting.

Planning the Meeting

Traditional practice provides a standard plan for the presiding officer. As noted earlier, unless the organization adopts a special order of business, this is the sequence of events:

1. Call to order
2. Reading of the minutes of the last meeting
3. Reports of standing committees
4. Reports of special committees
5. Unfinished business from previous meetings
6. New business
7. Miscellaneous: announcements, requests, items, etc.
8. Adjournment

The astute chairman will flesh out this skeleton with notes on his own outline concerning the committees he knows will be ready to report, and the order in which he will call upon them; the items of unfinished business as reflected in the secretary's minutes, and the order in which they should be considered; and such new business as he can anticipate. Whenever practicable the chairman will see that an agenda, incorporating these additional items, is circulated to members in advance, knowing that more thoughtful discussion is apt to result when members have had an opportunity to think about problems ahead of time.

Conducting the Meeting

At this point the presiding officer may need the wisdom of Solomon, the patience of Job, and the tenacity of Joshua. Lesser men, as most chairman are, must settle for as much common sense as they can muster. Aside from the detailed process of handling motions and knowing proper forms—matters he should be willing to master as a minimum qualification for his post— the presiding officer can command the confidence and respect of his assembly by adhering to these simple rules, cheerfully, tactfully, and firmly:

1. Call the meeting to order on time, and proceed with the usual order of business if a quorum is present.

2. Keep the meeting in order at all times: one motion, one speaker, and amity for all.

3. Decide all parliamentary questions, with advice from the parliamentarian whenever necessary. But remember that any decision may be appealed from by two members and subjected to a majority vote of the assembly.

4. Preside impersonally, even referring to himself as "the chair," and refraining from expressing personal opinions on questions before the assembly, or showing personal bias when giving information or making rules.

5. State each motion (or have the secretary read it), after it has been seconded, and then call for discussion. After discussion

restate the motion before taking a vote. Announce the results after every vote. (Especially in large meetings, it is desirable to stand up when stating the motion, putting the question, and announcing the vote, though remaining seated during discussion.)

6. Recognize persons asking for the floor, giving preference to those who have not previously spoken, and alternating among those holding differing views on the question under discussion.

7. If he must speak to the motion, or for other reasons wishes to leave the chair, ask the vice-president or some other officer to take charge of the meeting.

8. Cast a vote on a pending motion only to break a tie, or to make one.

Evaluating the Meeting

Some form of evaluation of each meeting will be helpful in improving the next one. A brief conference among the officers of the organization (including the "opposition" leaders in a two-party situation), will usually suffice to indicate ways of increasing the efficiency of the assembly without sacrificing its democracy. Occasionally all members of the group may profitably be invited to state their reactions to the way in which the meeting was conducted.

V

CONSTITUTIONS AND BYLAWS

As members participate in business meetings and as presiding officers chair them, questions commonly arise which can be settled only by reference to the basic code of the organization. This code often consists of a single document; at other times it includes several. Reference should be made to some of the volumes listed in "VI. Suggested Readings" for detailed procedures on the steps in forming permanent organizations, including the drawing up of basic codes. For the purposes of this manual we can only summarize the nature and function of the basic code, and outline the kinds of information it contains.

A *constitution* is the most common basic document. As in the case of our federal government, it is the supreme authority of the organization. As such it sets forth the basic principles and general structure of the organization. It is drawn up and adopted by the founders of the organization and is usually difficult to amend. In the case of corporate bodies this document is called a *charter* or *articles of incorporation*.

Bylaws are rules which establish the detailed procedures necessary to carry out or put into practice the provisions of the constitution. Where the constitution is general, the bylaws are specific. The constitution, for example, may name the officers of an organization, but the bylaws prescribe the way in which they are to be chosen. Generally, the separate provisions of the bylaws parallel those of the constitution. Because they stand below the constitution in a table of authority, the bylaws are usually easier to amend.

Standing rules cover matters that are less important than those contained in the constitution or bylaws, but ones which are essential to the functioning of the organization: the time and place of meeting, the order of business, limitations on the number and length of speeches, and so on. Ordinarily these portions of the basic code are the easiest to amend.

Rules of order are also part of the basic code and cover all matters not provided for in the constitution, bylaws, or standing rules. These rules are sometimes referred to as the *parliamentary authority,* officially adopted by the organization. Thus this manual of the essentials of parliamentary procedure might be designated as "the parliamentary authority for all matters not covered in the constitution and bylaws."

In most voluntary associations modern practice is to combine the constitution and bylaws into a single document. Whether the basic code consists of one or two documents, these are the provisions normally included:

    I. NAME OF THE ORGANIZATION
   II. PURPOSE OF THE ORGANIZATION
      A. General statement of objects
      B. General means of attaining the purpose
  III. MEMBERSHIP
      A. Qualifications
      B. Separate classes of members (if any)
      C. Method of selection
      D. Dues
  IV. OFFICERS
      A. Designation by name and duties

    B. Term of office

    C. Method of election

V. EXECUTIVE BOARD AND COMMITTEES

    A. Membership of board (if any), and how constituted

    B. Designation of standing committees and duties

    C. Procedure for establishing special committees

    D. Method of selection of committee members and chairmen

VI. MEETINGS

    A. Frequency of regular meetings

    B. Procedure for calling special meetings

    C. Definition of a quorum

VII. AMENDMENT

    A. Method of amendment

    B. Vote required

Occasionally the matters ordinarily covered by standing rules, and the designation of a parliamentary authority, are also included in a single document with the bylaws. In such cases they can usually be found under the provision dealing with meetings.

VI

SUGGESTED READINGS

For the reader who wishes to supplement this discussion of the essentials of parliamentary procedure the following sources are recommended:

Adult Education Association of the U.S.A., *Streamlining Parliamentary Procedure* (Chicago, 1957), a symposium by Knowles, English, O'Brien, Tacey, Auer, Mason, and Sturgis, reprinted from *Adult Leadership*, December, 1956, pp. 177–193.

CUSHING, Luther Stearns, *Cushing's Manual of Parliamentary Practice,* rev. by Albert S. Bolles (Philadelphia, The John C. Winston Company, 1947).

JONES, O. G., *Senior Manual for Group Leadership,* rev. ed. (New York, Appleton-Century-Crofts, Inc., 1949).

O'BRIEN, Joseph F., *Parliamentary Law for the Layman* (New York, Harper & Brothers, 1952).

ROBERT, Henry M., *Rules of Order Revised,* 75th anniversary ed. (Chicago, Scott, Foresman and Company, 1951).

STURGIS, Alice B., *Sturgis Standard Code of Parliamentary Procedure* (New York, McGraw-Hill Book Company, Inc., 1950).

INDEX

CLASSIFICATION OF MOTIONS ACCORDING TO PRECEDENCE

	Second needed?	Amendable?	Debatable?	Required vote	Interrupt speaker?
Privileged motions					
(in order of precedence)					
Fix time of next meeting	yes	yes	no[3]	½	no
Adjourn	yes	no	no	½	no
Recess	yes	yes	no[3]	½	no
Question of privilege	no	no	no	ch.[2]	yes
Subsidiary motions					
(in order of precedence)					
Lay on the table	yes	no	no	½	no
Previous question	yes	no	no	⅔	no
Limit debate	yes	yes	no	⅔	no
Postpone to a certain time ...	yes	yes	yes	½	no
Refer to committee	yes	yes	yes	½	no
Committee of the whole	yes	yes	yes	½	no
Amend	yes	yes	[1]	½	no
Postpone indefinitely	yes	no	yes	½	no
Main motions					
(no order of precedence)					
Main motion for general business	yes	yes	yes	½	no
Take from the table	yes	no	no	½	no
Reconsider	yes	no	[1]	½	yes
Rescind	yes	yes	yes	⅔	no
Make special order of business	yes	yes	yes	⅔	no
Incidental motions					
(no order of precedence)					
Point of order	no	no	no	ch.[3]	yes
Appeal from decision of chair	yes	no	[1]	½	yes
Suspend rules	yes	no	no	⅔	no
Object to consideration	no	no	no	⅔	yes
Parliamentary inquiry	no	no	no	ch.	yes
Request for information	no	no	no	ch.	yes
Withdraw a motion	no	no	no	½	no

[1] Debatable only when the motion to which it is applied was debatable.
[2] Requires only chair's decision; majority vote if appealed from chair.
[3] Original motion not debatable; amendment debatable.

NOTE: ½ means one more than half of those voting (simple majority); ⅔ means two thirds of those voting.

CLASSIFICATION OF SPECIAL MOTIONS ACCORDING
TO PURPOSE

	Second needed?	Amend- able?	Debat- able?	Required vote	Interrupt speaker?
To suppress debate or hasten action					
1. Previous question	yes	no	no	$\frac{2}{3}$	no
2. Suspend rules	yes	no	no	$\frac{2}{3}$	no
3. Limit debate	yes	yes	no	$\frac{2}{3}$	no
4. Take from the table	yes	no	no	$\frac{1}{2}$	no
5. Make special order of business	yes	yes	yes	$\frac{2}{3}$	no
To delay action					
6. Postpone to a certain time	yes	yes	yes	$\frac{1}{2}$	no
7. Lay on the table	yes	no	no	$\frac{1}{2}$	no
8. Refer to committee	yes	yes	yes	$\frac{1}{2}$	no
To prevent action					
9. Object to consideration .	no	no	no	$\frac{2}{3}$	yes
10. Withdraw a motion	no	no	no	$\frac{1}{2}$	no
11. Postpone indefinitely . . .	yes	no	yes	$\frac{1}{2}$	no
To consider more carefully					
12. Committee of the whole .	yes	yes	yes	$\frac{1}{2}$	no
To change a decision					
13. Reconsider	yes	no	[1]	$\frac{1}{2}$	yes
14. Rescind	yes	yes	yes	$\frac{2}{3}$	no
To maintain rules and order					
15. Question of privilege . . .	no	no	no	ch.[2]	yes
16. Point of order	no	no	no	ch.[2]	yes
17. Appeal from decision of chair	yes	no	[1]	$\frac{1}{2}$	yes
18. Parliamentary inquiry . .	no	no	no	ch.	yes
19. Request for information .	no	no	no	ch.	yes
To close a meeting					
20. Adjourn	yes	no	no	$\frac{1}{2}$	no
21. Fix time of next meeting	yes	yes	no[3]	$\frac{1}{2}$	no
22. Recess	yes	yes	no[3]	$\frac{1}{2}$	no

[1] Debatable only when the motion to which it is applied was debatable.

[2] Requires only chair's decision; majority vote if appealed from chair.

[3] Original motion not debatable; amendment debatable.

NOTE: $\frac{1}{2}$ means one more than half of those voting (simple majority); $\frac{2}{3}$ means two thirds of those voting.